The Dark Side of the Divine

Poetry by E. Elizabeth Gray

The Dark Side of the Divine
Copyright ©2024 E. Elizabeth Gray
Cover Image- William Jackson

All rights reserved. Blue Jade Press, LLC retains the right to reprint this book. Permission to reprint poems from this collection must be obtained by the author.

ISBN- 978-1-961043-04-6

Published by:

Blue Jade Press, LLC

Blue Jade Press, LLC
Vineland, NJ 08360
www.bluejadepress.com

Acknowledgements

Long ago, with a thousand shades of the universe in my head and behind my eyes, a girl too brilliantly mad to be inspired by the shallow nature of the rite of high school scribbled wild stories on loose-leaf paper folded into little triangles and slid across scuffed floors - the texts of Generation X retrieved by dear friends who loved to laugh while reading them. We barely survived, but I remember, when one said to me, "You should write a book." The words remained a challenge that I've heard many times over many years that now seem like a lifetime. And so finally, I did.

It is imperative that I first thank my husband, Shawn. Thanks for giving me free rein to chase my adventures. To Austin my oldest son, who changed the entire course of my life, you will ever be my personal Superhero who gave me the will to survive. To Thomas, my youngest son, my Angel, you made everything broken within me whole again. My breath and my blood, thank you for putting up with the hours lost while I scrawled madly in my books. Thank you for believing I could.

Thank you Carrie for reading my folded-up notes and Jen for countless hours under the stars pondering life and listening to Cake and Tool. Together, we share the burden of our collective knowing through the bonds of *Sisterhood* over three decades in the fire service. Thank you for just knowing.

Thank you, Mom and Sarah, for enduring hours of talking about "the book."

Many thanks to The Maryland Writer's Association for the platform to read my work and for giving me the courage to call myself a writer.

Special thanks to Rebecca and Blue Jade Press for taking a chance on me and giving me this opportunity and the time to navigate all the feelings.

Thank you to *The Poet*, who once told me to write through my feelings and for showing me how to turn pain into prose.

There is no greater acknowledgment than that owed to a very special friend, who inspired the first work of mine ever read before an audience: a poem inspired by his unexpected loss during the dark months of COVID. There is the deepest connection shared between all firemen - the bonds of the brotherhood and through our collective sorrow and trauma, in the spirit of our service and the sacrifices that haunt the shadows our memories and within the remembrances of all the names we hold in eternal reverence, our mentors, our colleagues, our friends, ourselves, your light shines on. Thank you Richard "Dickie" Atwell, Jr.

Finally, to my steadfast friends, the hunter Orion and a little flower named Lucy you are always there for me.

For Dickie
For all first responders who carry the darkness within
For Donna
For all little girls who dream of being more
And dare to take it

Table of Contents

Storyteller	1
Disclaimer	3
Artemis and the Hunter	5
Songbird	6
Divine Feminine	8
The Accidental Whisper	11
Remember Always	14
Divining	16
Celestial	17
Old Friend	18
Red Tea Pot	19
Shearing Day	20
Just Another Dream	22
Who Are You?	23
Wild	24
Conquered	28
Unspoken	30
Expendable	31
Moment	32
What I Know About Cats	33
Wild Thing	35
The Green Coat	37
Perspective	39
Self…	40
Empty	41
Loneliness	42
The Mariner	44
What do I Know	45
Roadkill	47
Grandmother	50
Playing the Odds with Strangers	51
Good Morning	52
I Took a Chance	53
Sensory	54
Kindness	59
What Color are your Eyes	61
The River	62
How a Soldier Hides	64

Drowning	66
Balloons	68
Bloodletting	69
To Her Friend, the Poet	71
The Canvas	73
There's No Goddess of Hope	74
Hiraeth	75
Tick Tock	79
Impasto	80
Anatomy of the Heart	83
Niosh F2000-13	87
Senior Living Shades of Green	91
Reverberation	93
Flowers	96
Gardenias	98
Morning Glories	102
The Mountain	106

Storyteller

I am a storyteller
not a writer or poet or painter or bard
I belong around a fire
with unruly children at my feet
in a tribal circle
I am a mediocre version
of Socrates under a tree
my genre is the aesthetic
my form, the rise and fall of the voice
the ebb and flow of the theme and metaphor
the passion of my ancestors
the stories of my people whittled and modeled
like wood left in the rain swelling with each retelling
always true to the spirit of the teller
it is pressed charcoal
or oil paint (some shade of umber)
staining fingers
it is wispy lines on a blank canvas
and music and silence and wind in the leaves
the bubbling of water as the river flows endlessly
to wherever it goes
like a story unfolds

I am a storyteller
no iteration of Guttenberg can print me
no illumination can recreate me
no blinking cursor
drowning in blue light and pixels
my words are not confined
by Webster and Roget's
fuck the grammar of the lingua franca
I am not cheapened by the limitations of typeset and font
by pages and chapters and volume
no editor will scratch red carets slashes or notes
in my margins.

I breathe
I pulse
and not like the cursor in its little box
I will be no slave to the forum
or feed
or clips
or reel

You should take great care not to cheapen me
by placing value in my silence
for I will find a different ear
even if it must be a tree, a squirrel, or the stars

I cannot be frozen and fixed in books of myth and legend
or runes or pictographs
with those things you cut off my voice
and the stories will die
as the stories of all the ancients have died before me
I am a yarn in a blanket of threads
woven by generations of storytellers
carefully stitched and loved
wrapped up and passed on
through spoken language
the oral histories of the universe
not a tweet or a snap
or even all of the tomes of all of the greatest libraries
could ever hold me
or any card catalog
or microfiche
or fucking Google

None will ever hold the power
or capture all of the words
and nuance of the storyteller
for I am a storyteller
and I will no longer be ashamed of it

Disclaimer

I am not a poet
a writer
an artist
a musician
I am none of those things

I am just a silly girl
with discount dollar store
knock-off trauma
the crack is real
but the vessel is of little value
it cannot be compared

I am just an old woman
with a thousand selfies on her phone
in search of just one redeeming quality
because I know
the world places more value on the curve of a tit
than the bends of a mind

So, don't look my way
I'm only screaming my madness
in ink on paper
and scratching it out
in angry black scribbles smeared with tears
and there is remorse for all the lost pseudo-prose
what have I done
in the throes of my madness?

I'm only saying
that I am not what you imagine
and I am not what I imagine either
I do not seek rhyme
or meter
or snobbery
defined by a fine art pedigree

There is no virtuoso in my
pencil scribed insanity
I am rebellious to
conventions of punctuation
and overuse of the fucking exclamation point
or the word fuck!

I want you to know when I am screaming
I want you to know that I am breathing
I want you to know this is the end

But who am I?
Who knows?
I just know I am not a poet
(but maybe I am)

Artemis and the Hunter

Stoic hunter sentry over somber indigo
longing she gazed upon her shimmering fancy
unveiled piercing arrow of Artemis, sorrow

Constant companion abandoned to fallow
innocent daughter of no man or kin she seeks
the stoic hunter sentry over somber indigo

If longing alone could bring heat to wintry shadow
she'd gaze chin upturned for all of eternity
unveiled piercing arrow of Artemis, sorrow

Why must innocents suffer love's incurable woe
she keens to the silvery pinpoints of heaven
to the stoic hunter sentry over somber indigo

Won't you move just once diverge from the farrow
penance anchored to pitch of gloom your sin, being
unveiled piercing arrow of Artemis, sorrow

Lamenting eyes bound 'til sun brings the morrow
she fades as her fancy abandons her sky
the stoic hunter sentry over somber indigo
unveiled piercing arrow of Artemis, sorrow

Song Bird

What a lovely garden for a songbird
unsullied by shame
brilliant, feathered breast
the haunting tweet-twitter of an angel
she sings
and all must love her

Don't you? Love her?

Shade cloaks the garden
like the silly daydreams
of tittering daisies
that aspire to be roses
she can't see joyful yellow in the black
so the black becomes the joy

Don't fret, child
there is providence in suffering
fuck innocence
trade up for shame
sacrifice paves the road to the good life

Didn't you know?
Didn't you?

Perched upon her branch
without a stitch of dignity
she notices
or the first time
the flush of red
across her cold breast

She covers herself coyly
she welcomes the shadow
harmony becomes dissonance
the songbird
sings a song
of silence

Can't you hear?
Isn't she lovely?

What a lovely songbird
seen but not heard
flesh concealed and voice silenced
to nittering nods of approval
encore! encore!
and she thinks the world must love her

Don't you? Love her?

Divine Feminine

Jagged mouth of granite
boulders, like Zen stacked stones
the shoulders of Magna Mater
when she was still strong
and revered
woman resides inside her yawn
her cave

Reverberation in cold metamorphic slate of gray
whispers of wind and water
murmur, *Cebele*
your place is here
but a woman is color and heat
when the world is at her feet
infants suckle
when the world is at her hip
man, hypnotized
gives seed to first-born son and sibling
borne of an act called "love"
though it feels more like duty
as the world at last drifts away
as babes become men
as utility fades

The idol they worshipped, Gaia
that mother is fertile
not feral
she is milk giver
she is vessel for man's need
or maybe vassal
or maybe chattel
she is sex
until she is not

Color fades
a lump of clay, stone and bone
tossed in a trash heap
and buried for all time
until Uruk is finally rediscovered
and the modern mothers
so passionate in their desires to be revered
-rejoiced

Oh! she must have been a goddess
so many idols in the sand
but no foolish woman,
she was merely a vessel
filled up and used
until she could hold no more
and tossed into the refuse

Gray haired,
wrapped in wrinkled crepe
blue blood pulsing beneath
the naked eye can see
she is no goddess
but mortal woman
and they look away disappointed
or was it pity
or the discomfort of seeing their own future

In the silence of abandonment
she slinks into the shadows
silent sentry over her creations
until even that utility becomes sadness
and shame
she looks to the mountain
relieved that it has no mirrors

Into the granite she fades
into the folded arms of Magna Mater
swallowed into the gut
settled betwixt the stone cold breast
and petrified womb
soothing herself with
dreams of cooing babes
who no longer need a mother

The whispers of wind and water
murmur, be at peace *Cebele*
my child
your place is here now
and so she breathes out slowly
and turns to stone

The Accidental Whisper

One day
quite by accident
while resting under a tree
a whisper met a breeze
even Aristotle would have paused
to ponder such a thing
and the whisper hitched a ride on the breeze
embarking upon a journey
to find as many ears as it could

The whisper found comfort
in the endless ebb and flow
of the breeze's course
soft and gentle currents
meandering farther and farther from the tree
and with each warm updraft and cool descent
the breeze found comfort in companionship

A breeze never stays in one place for long
and a whisper never travels far
so upon mutual necessity
they traveled together
spinning, lazy and free
the whisper and the breeze

The breeze
she was gentle and kind
although born from a storm
and the whisper
he was jaded and restrained
to each other
they were hope
of something different
of something more

Despite her chaotic origin
and peripatetic nature
and having no voice of her own
that one would hear
the breeze instead gave her soul
embracing fantasy
as the breeze was wont to do
she was happy to oblige
the whisper

Alas, by chance
or fatalistic irony
the whisper was too loud
in his own ears
and he would not hear
and the breeze lamented that
he could not find his own heart

Saddened, the breeze
remained true
propelled by her turbulence
accommodating the whisper
and calling it, trust
and the whisper knew
the breeze would never let him down hard
or abandon him

For the whisper knows
how to charm the senses
how to catch a ride
on a lonely breeze
how to find an ear
and upon finding one
how to leave

But, the breeze
having given many rides
to countless cold whispers
always knew he would abandon her
filling himself with her
and giving nothing
still she hoped

The breeze finally slowed
descending to rest
on a vista of terracotta rocks
near a tranquil azure sea
like watercolors soaked into
thick fibered parchment
the tinkering of a gentle tide upon
the smooth ancient pebbles
of knowledge and time
and there the whisper did depart
in search of solitude

The breeze bid farewell to her Apollo
before catching the sails of
the Kato Mylos
and she soared to that height
where drops of salted tears
never reach the earth
for she already knew solitude
only begets sorrow
foolish whisper

Had he noticed
Aristotle might have shed a tear
to ponder it but alas
he too would eventually rise
dust the dirt off his cloak
and walk away whispering to himself
no longer intrigued by a departed breeze
for the whisper is a man
and a breeze a mere remnant
of a long silenced storm

Remember Always

Remember always
you are a rock
you've been here
for what seemed like centuries
unmoved except by
great calamity
but still here

And as each day
passes into night
giving way to beautiful sunrise
frozen over many winters
yet thawed each spring
moss has grown upon you

From time to time
you've given shade
and shelter
to other living things
in need of respite
and yet
you've weathered
many storms

This is not to say you're unchanged
you are changed
you've been etched slowly
by wind and rain
pieces have fallen away
as you've frozen and thawed
like tears can scar your heart
yet the sun still warms you
and you're still here

You've been covered by great floods
and tumbled by earthquakes
geologic forces
threaten to destroy you
small pieces of you
washed away in the storm
out to sea
to some other destiny
yet the moon still shines
and you're still here

And as the stars danced across night skies
this road weary traveler
found your rock among many
and upon you
chose you to take a rest
and she is glad for it

Divining

The espresso machine
hisses at me each morning
as I gently pour the steamed milk
into the black heart of
whatever cup suits my sentimental whimsy

Swirling like there is
a purpose
to the turn of my wrist
conducting a masterpiece
rather than a cup of coffee
in a chipped mug with the handle glued back on

Staring at the cheap press espresso
in hue of burnt umber
mingle with the milk
as if I am divining the swirls of the cream
against the foamy head

What is my future
except some lie I tell myself
to make believe
I am not just another animal
with an afterlife mantra
chanted frantically with clasped hands
in the darkness of night and day
to keep from screaming
against the hiss in my own head

Only there is no swirly sweet cream for divining
there is only the fact
that we will all die alone
and only the worms and the vultures
will rejoice

Celestial

The moon and the stars
are my only true friends
always in their places
always willing to listen
even if it is not by choice
they never hide for long
and they never leave
on the surface
it may seem similar to a text
read and replied to
at first
then overtime
a longer latency
fewer replies
now unread at all
hanging in silent impotency
like my stars hang in the sky
waiting to be noticed
and someday, I suppose
when I've tired of waiting
of trying
I will let you fade away
like the waning gibbous moon
fades to quarter
then crescent
and then disappears altogether
only I do not turn on an axis
if I am your moon
I will fade away forever
and so the moon and stars
are my steadfast friends
I don't get to hear
their voices or yours
but if they could
they'd probably tell me
to just be quiet

Old Friend

Old friend the moon
steadfast and true
guiding Artemis
to her hunter in the sky
wishing she could fly away
and hide in the blanket of the universe
peeking through the holes
of a constellation called sorrow
her story regret
her tragedy
wasted time
her sin (she whispers)
ego sum

Red Tea Pot

Disappointment is
like loose tea leaves
steeped too long
in lukewarm water
no longer palatable
acrid and bitter upon the tongue
but if one is thirsty enough
they will force themselves to drink

The lie she tells herself
is that the trademarked teabag
from the yellow box
with string and stapled tag
wrapped in a paper envelope
is something less refined
than that which is measured carefully
from a fancy tin
unique and infused
although with certainty floating free
in the heavy cast iron tea pot
enameled red
the same substance as medieval chains
shackles poured into a different mold
but the tea leaves
all come from the same place
they aren't so fancy after all

Disappointment is the realization
that whether you drink "gourmet" tea
or you're strong and turn away
the shackles remain
while tea leaves and tears
float in the dark amber water
you swallow
like a good girl
fill the pot
and add more leaves

Shearing Day

Shorn from flesh
once warm now cold
pulled, manipulated
from the soft pillowed tufts
that once cradled the heads of kindred and kin

No longer some unruly thing
no longer "alive"
inanimate blob
uncontained by straps and bands
stuffed into burlap sacks
graded then sold
dipped into boiling vats of vinegar
steeped in madder, weld or woad
and Tyrian purple, the color of royalty

Another hapless creature molested and marketed
essences squeezed out
for the pleasure of others
extracted by army and empire
pontiff and king
priceless when compared
to the humble mollusk or beast from whence it came

Wool pulled by calloused, numbed hands
into a fine strands
twined together and spun
with stone-faced deception
the yarn is soft, yet itchy upon virgin skin

Although for all of the work
the tragedy is that you were soft in the first place
with the sweet smell of lanolin
but, rejoice!
now you have "utility" rolled into clever skeins
merchandized, commercialized
no longer a pastoral thing
rather a "commodity"

What is your actual worth today
unwelcome hands caressing
eyes discerning
and if chosen pulled, slowly
twisted and woven
into someone else's dream

Just Another Dream

Warm fingertips
trace lazy circles
on a bronzed shoulder
no words spoken
none needed
calming her wildness
she breathes in the cadence
of the caress
desire
caution
a shoulder is safe
to cry on
to lean on
or more dangerously
a place to start the great unraveling
something savage
lust
need
nerve endings firing
on skin that screams
more
and begs silently
please never leave

Who Are You?

Who are you?
you're every fucking flaw
real or imagined
you're a lifeguard in the stand
too much sun
in a thin slip of red and blue Lycra
overexposed
hiding that fat roll
that makes you hate yourself more
and the wrinkles
the crape-y skin
swelling knuckles
old, old, old
the emptiness of future desires
given or taken
always looking out
watching over everyone else
saving everyone else
loving everyone else
who watches over you
no one
by design
lost in obscurity
but maybe someday
many years later they'll say
whatever came of that girl?
nothing

Wild

He came through the door
wild, like a lion
looking for his next kill
his next meal
eat or be eaten
kill or be killed
hind brain throwing roadblocks
frontal lobe disengaged

He's mistaken
shame
cynicism
and self-loathing
for passion
he engages his lips
teeth bared
she is pinned against his wall
he miscalculated her
teeth
and claws
and brute strength
magnetism
no- confidence
he thinks that he is in control
that he controls her
he's misjudged
her animal

She was borne
of a lifetime
disappointment
and distrust
she saw
through him
on day one

Foolish
she wanted
a different narrative
and so she tried
to mold it
like a fucking lump of clay
turns into a beautiful urn
-or some shit like that

She would call him
"favorite"
and inevitably
smash him to a million pieces
on the kitchen floor

She let him
pin her
she let his
lips explore
before the door
slammed shut

She knew he would
so she'd slam it first

Her value?
tits and a blow job
that is what kept him up at night
after all

And so she gave into him
right there
her very best performance
"Oscar" worthy
to the end

And to his extreme pleasure
courtesy warning ignored
she proceeded to the encore

And while he licked
the blood and sinew of victory
from his paw
while he reveled
sated and high
from the release
she stood and put her shirt back on
wiping him off her face

Her mask on
eyes afire of green
avoiding shame
a lie
well-rehearsed

He asked
"what about you?"
(his conscience, not his desire)
she replied
while walking away
"what about me?"

And just before the bathroom door shut
and the lock engaged
she turned and
waved her hand
like swatting at a fly

As the water turned on
he shrugged his shoulders
tucked himself back into his pants
and he left
he got what he came for
she knew he would

Standing in the steamy shower
a little more weary
a little less human
if there were tears
they were hidden in the steam
as she touched herself
bringing her own release
alone like a woman

Conquered

I heard you breathe
I heard you sigh
and I realized that you are torment

I heard you say my name
and realized it was my reward
I heard your sadness
and realized perhaps I was wrong

No, not wrong
I've just lost my own way
preparing for a storm
I don't know how to navigate

Maybe this is how the Phoenicians felt
as they ventured across the sea
in reed boats with meager provisions
and dreams

Maybe this is how Columbus felt
or the first brave Vikings
on voyages south,
or your grandfather

Or you

Those brave souls
with only stars
and neither compass
nor chart to guide them

Bravery,
seeking fortune, seeking glory
forging ahead
into unknown water

Walking unknown lands
tasting unknown fruit
deciphering unknown tongues
and it must have been worth it

For they returned
again and again
like you
to me

This is how I feel
when I hear you breathe
I feel utterly conquered

Unspoken

You were exceptional
You were a light
You included everyone
even the awkward girl
on "the apron"
the one no others included

Things we should have whispered to the dead
-while they were living

Expendable

Sometimes she feels expendable
like those little 8-count boxes of crayons
you know all the colors
you think they can't create beauty
unless they are neat and new
but one is broken
the others peeled and rounded from overuse
they are no longer shiny
or new
the wax stinks
and 99 cents yields a brand-new box

Moment

Some people are meant for just a moment,
like young lovers sitting on a diving board
bare feet dangling in Florida February
that felt like Maryland May
the pulse of the breeze echoed
in the lazy slap of the weir against the skimmer
sounds a pool makes in the night
under a shimmering moon
and the other watchful guardians of the sky
tender lips that made no promises
just two beings who found each other
for a moment in a turbulent world
daring to dream
then parted at dawn
I don't even remember your name
but I remember the sweet taste of your kiss
and gentle caress
perhaps I still crave the simplicity of it

What I Know About Cats

Some cats
can love you silly
and never stop
some cats
you must win over
and it takes time
some cats
are feral creatures
with no reason to need you
you must show them how to trust
as predation and parasite abound
you must make them see
you were created to love them
and there will always be a warm box by the door
a glorious tin of wet smelly tuna
cool clean water
in a whimsical ceramic dish
lazy fingers softly stroking behind notched ears
tempered and tagged and maintained
wild they are
and yet they crave
a human unafraid
to touch a wild thing
(the cat or maybe a man)
seems an impossible thing
as they sit apart
staring sideways through slits for eyes
wary of kindness
wary of love
yet there is always a yearning
as the box
becomes the foot of the bed
then the lap
and then your heart betrays your soul
what I know about cats
is that it takes a long time
on the cat's level
it takes so many soft-spoken promises

and broken ones too
so many treats and tributes
unreturned
confused by the heart of an animal
whose only real inclination is
to find food and security
and to be a good Hobbesian
or die trying
wary of their own kind
to never let their guard down
for a promise of easy food
and warmth
the promise of a companion
for life
and so the real obstacle
for the cat (and a man)
is to overcome
the ego
the I
the me

Wild Thing

A wild thing will often hide
necessity born of evolutionary victories
one escape at a time
its father wasn't eaten
and therefore its genetic code wins
and it passes on the liberty to cower
to all generations beyond
but it still bled

When his heart beat like a tympani
the soldier learned to breathe
instead of learning to run and hide
perhaps he remarked on the beauty of a doe
as he slowed his heart
to the dullest thud
numb enough to squeeze the trigger

The wild thing falls and red stains its tawny hide
blending into the brown grass and underbrush
soldier and prey are not so different after all
one evades the hunter
the other, love

The soldier will infiltrate, stalk, and strike
he is steadfast in his role as protector
of the family
of the faith
but who protects him?

The prey, she skulks in the shadows
cradling dreams of impossibility
she doesn't know how to trust anyone or herself
She dances in the shadows of the trees
beneath the stars
cursing the bondage chains
of the sacred feminine

Wild things
constrained by tropes and constructs
when really, they just want to fuck

The Green Coat

Coveted through the storefront glass
wool peacoat of muted pine
one month of pasta, beans or ramen
four weeks of gasoline
half a month's rent
-a tiny room with shared bathroom
and kitchen privileges
warmth was expensive
but the coat was worth it
charged on a brand new credit card
a responsible thing
a practical thing

You saw the coat
"what a hideous drape"
"hobo" you said
a hobo is a homeless person
but home is supposed
to be where heart and family reside

I still love you though
even as you thought me foolish
to waste good money on living
no —subsisting
while you lived in a great house
with a great veranda
with azaleas
perfect for entertaining

You thought me foolish
the coat garish
with too many adjectives
ending in ish
you would not be seen with me
in that coat

And with hurt
disguised as anger
and for your viewing pleasure
I gifted the coat
to a dumpster
also shades of green
painted steel and rust

Across yonder lot
casting its shadow
stinking of refuse
just like me
whilst in frigid swirling wind
we crossed the mall parking lot
to spend obscene amounts
of your money
on Christmas gifts
that would never keep me warm

I always loved father
but I also loved my green coat
it kept me warm
when I was cold and alone
but I was not enough to keep it
I loved my pride more
I craved his approval more
even now dressed up pretty for my father's sake now
my heart still rots, soil stained
in piles of refuse
within a rusted receptacle of distaste
as I shiver in winter
unwanted and never enough

Perspective

Bowline
Square Knot
Becket Bend
Clove Hitch
Figure-Eight

He sees domination
She sees empowerment

Self…

self-care
self-help
self-sufficient
self- ish
self-management
self-absorbed
sado masochist (self-harm)
self-healing
self-talk (stupid, ugly, worthless)
self-worth
self-image
self-made
self-conscious
self-evident
self-pity
self-pity
self-pity
"…to thine own self be true*…"
self-actualization?
actually,
self-repudiation
self-defense
steel yourself
self-esteem
self-efficacy (erupts in laughter)
self-loathing
self-reliant
self-satisfying
self "love" (shameful you lust-filled sinner)
self-possessed
self-induced
self-enucleate
self-flagellation
self-immolation
self-fulfilling prophecy
self-destruct

* Shakespeare, William, 1564-1616 author. The Tragedy of *Hamlet*, 1.3 (78-80) Prince of Denmark. [London] :The Folio Society, 1954

Empty

Empty space is not empty
I am a particle in a vacuum
of nothing but myself
while I walk and smile for the audience

Loneliness

Loneliness
is knowing
the deafening
silence
of clarity
reflecting back at you
like beams of light in a fog

Burning that never penetrates
layers of glare obscuring
the road ahead
forcing you to down shift
swallowing your vision
in a cloak of eerie mist

The twin yellow lines
you will follow
trusting they will guide you
as they bend into
the opaque morass
of your dreams
imagined destinations
compete with the electronic glow
of the gps map

North, feels like lost to me

Artificial fluorescent
light emitting diodes
are no substitute for the sun
which can burn
away the fog
bronze pale cheeks
sanitize the linens
or grow seeds
from the compost
of what once was
all by mid-morning

High beams refracting
off a billion particles of water and light
but no warmth
and none can see by it

Man made light
faux like friends
on the friends list
like followers and thumbs up
little emoji hearts and smiles
pixels for people

LOL

Always beaming back
never penetrating
refracting more shallow than a platitude
screaming
and not being heard
crying
and no longer hiding
behind sunglasses
from the recesses
of a well-loved hoodie

Speaking a language
no other speaks
of innuendo and metaphor
buried deep in the mud
like a cephalopod
words compressed to the extinction
of logic

Because truth
makes people
uncomfortable
they don't want it

But I do

The Mariner

The soul weary mariner gazed upon the fickle sea
hiding behind heart compass without true north
hoping he finds his shore for all eternity

Swells of tears and brine sting sun leathered cheek
utility masqueraded as love, fire lost o're stretch of time
and the soul weary mariner gazed upon the fickle sea

Words stained in ink of poem and play - his story finally free
an unexpected mermaid swims near and earns his smile
hoping he finds his shore for all eternity

Standing upon oft-scrubbed deck the ghost of an ancient tree that never dreamed of the sea
like chart and sextant plot courses not so linear as cypress or pine
still, the soul weary mariner gazed upon the fickle sea

For hope? For love? For redemption- to the wind of the heavens he raised his plea
and the mermaid sighed sweet breaths to fill his sails
(she dreams with a single tear)
hoping he finds his shore for all eternity

Land ho! He cried sinking to penitent knee
curious, he turned blue jade eyes toward the glisten of the mermaid's curving breast
the soul weary mariner gazed upon the fickle sea
hoping he finds his shore for all eternity

What do I Know

Every line reflecting in the mirror
fading like a fickle morning mist
dissipates with the strengthening sun
who am I
do I even know
did I ever know

Am I the sum of a childhood memory
a teenage trauma
a reckless, fearless twenty something
unwilling matriarch
principled puritan parent of young babes
a griffin reborn out of the conflagration

Am I a sage
turning my back on one life
walking a path with a lost boy
guiding with compassion and tolerance
hoping to be a good friend
hoping to win
love?

Am I a lover
do I even believe
have I always been such a liar
everything I know
seems to be more transparent each day
and I am no longer the person I thought I knew

I am a lost traveler
with a warm hand to hold today
and hopefully tomorrow
and they will call that sin
but being a woman as defined is not?

Tomorrow is the only reality that will not fade
somewhere between dreams and stubborn mindsets
enslaved to the tropes

The script is long outdated
is God is still a thing?
and family?
and heart?

What I am not
is just some masterpiece of mediocrity
gesso'd over
awash'd with a richer tone of sienna
so my colors don't shine through
what I am is a new canvas
awash'd in hope
a mind finally free
entwined within and about you

Roadkill

A deer carcass is no strange sight around here
the roads are littered year-round
I used to say a prayer for very little animal
angular death sculptures
on the side of the road

But I have grown more cynical
these days I'm just grateful
that it is cold outside
and I don't have smell the stench of death

A human smells different from an animal
I miss the innocence
I resent that I know the difference
between rotting man and beast

The mighty stag
an unrecognizable lump of pink matter
remnants of the hide that held it together
cast recklessly to the gravel shoulder
no bones
pulverized

I am mesmerized
by the total obliteration of such a large living thing
that which encounters a tractor-trailer
like a bug on a windshield
reduced to piles of formless matter

Not even enough left behind to stink
just a stain on the road
that makes you wince as your tires
grind into the guts
enough to remind

The pink stain
eventually carried away
by countless tire treads
or by a lucky late-night scavenger
persistent enough to scrape it off the road.
or wash'd away by rain
never to be pondered again

Hell of a way to go
no suffering
at least in this life
it's no different for a human
a different sort of animal
matter and hide and bone
we splat the same way

No one tries to put the deer back together
but, a man
we collect his parts
pretend we can make him whole again
or prepare him for burial
prescribing perpetual peace
or proscribing –nuance?

I know we would never leave that stain on the road
but I still see the stain
George made
his mark on the road
by the little white church
he didn't attend

What makes my lump of matter
any greater than the stag
staring at a pile of brain matter on the pavement
makes a good case for a seat belt
how absurd
that it was once encased
within a skull

A liberated mind
that had a name
memories and feelings
hopes and dreams
fear and love
a mother

Detritus dumped on the asphalt
I can't put it back
I can't leave it there
you can't just shovel him into the back of a pickup truck
or toss him in the woods for the worms
you can only shrug your shoulders and lie
"At least he didn't suffer."

Look at it
look at him
smell him and gingerly collect him
feel him slip over your gloves
tag him like game
be sure to document the evidence

Write a thorough report
make certain to add all the necessary details
that will haunt you for eternity
name
birthday
medical history
allergies
social security number (they've got to get paid)
primary complaint - really fucking dead

Why are we any different?
we bleed the same
we die the same
I doubt you could tell the difference
except maybe instead of a hide
you'd find blue jeans with twenty bucks in a pocket
fifty feet away from the pelvis
upon which it once rested

Grandmother

My grandmother
was the person most like me
except she never learned to drive
and all four of her children lived to be named
and she loved and feared God
she lived a virtuous life
she loved her husband and
he loved her

She gave me gardenias
and I have loved them since

Playing the Odds with Strangers

Sometimes
I walk slowly
through the city
alone
and late
in the night

And I do not look around
because silently
I am begging you
to shoot me in the head
to take my empty wallet

Sometimes
as you pass by
when I'm sitting on my bridge
I am begging
you to push me
to watch me fall
and then walk way

Sometimes
I scream
into the abyss
and all I hear is silence
yet my throat is still hoarse
from the screaming

Sometimes...

Good Morning

Good morning
a simple salutation
not like the ones required in a letter format
from armies of frauds
over a lifetime of tedious emails
"tack", "tack" "tacked" away
in a fluorescent lit hell of never ending paperwork
and mismatched office furniture
a metal desk that catches the arm of her chair
every time she jumps up to run away
a keyboard with an uncooperative "m" key
that often types "good mmmmorning"
thank god for the impersonalized utility of formats
to save her from awkward utterances in hallways
with averted eyes
because they caught her
and forced her to kindness
all the while thinking, Jesus I wish they'd go away

But how odd too
is a rare kind of utterance
that some other human
somewhere woke up and texted to me
a simple gesture that razed the walls of my fortress
and whispered "you are not alone"
in that context
a salutation brings the deepest smile
and in my darkest hours
of another tedious dawn
curiously, I returned
good morning to you too

I Took a Chance

You are resolute and immovable
yet I am willing to wait forever
if you wish it
and willing to go away
if you will it

I will never stop feeling
so much for you
although I may never find peace
in my turbulence
alone as I am

I haven't so many years left in me
and lo it doesn't matter
whether I ever find peace or not
yet it would be so sweet
and so I dream my greatest wish
to know your heart

Alas I am not worthy of the honor
I know
and you are not willing to give it
I know
for I am not the right one
I know
respect it I will
broken heart or not

So please understand
my transition is tumultuous
a thing in me is dying
whilst I rebuild my fortresses
not to keep you out
but to keep me in
I took a chance is all
I don't regret it

Sensory

Somewhere between longing and need
a wisp of hair brushed across a pallid cheek
summer bronze fleeting
as the sun slip'd further away from the day

The wisp, breaks her concentration
as a warm wind with a cool edge lifted
curls and spirits
a singular type of breeze

Not autumn, not winter
but the last kiss of warm sun
before the cold settles in
and becomes December

When the holidays pass
with the decorations
packed back in their boxes
when the lights no longer twinkle

Red and green
give way
to gray and gloom
and January comes as expected

A warm caress
short-lived, short-loved
then rain pushes the warmth of summer past
away for good

Bundling up in her black hoodie
she pondered the caress
of that perfect breeze
the way the wisp danced across her face

Wishing it was not
just an errant strand of hair
that never really wanted to touch her
what is a caress anyway?

Is it something
between a mother
easing her son's worry
and swatting away a gnat?

Or how a daughter
clings to her father's hand in his deathbed
gently rubbing to and fro
around thumb and fingers with a moistened towelette

Because that is what she watched
her aunt do
while guiding her father
to the afterlife

Did the universe send her this grief
so she would know how to handle it
when she was the daughter
and the body growing cold her own father

She was a good study of technique
mimicry not talent
duty, not love
love, not loved

Some caresses are much different
forbidden
erotic not like copulation
or even "making love"

Acts that inaccurately describe
the greater purpose of a caress
groping and probing
misnomered passion

Carnal
primitive
base, unless for darker reasons
unless for pleasure

Fornication
is just an act
of consummation
consumed of convolution

But a caress
itself is tantric
Andromeda unleashed
to all of the senses

What is a thumb
but a clumsy
stump of a digit
possessed of its own pulse

Yet drawn across the wrist
an inferno of nerves exposed
upon warm satiny skin
juxtaposed against the callused swirls and loops

Imagine it
so divine
drawn across the lips
more forbidden than the wrist

For the mouth says hurtful things
yet gives much pleasure
love or lies or whispered verses of a poet in your ear
it's all the same

Taste the carotid heat
pulsing against
an adventurous tongue
sweet torment

Rewarded with a sigh
as her breath catches
silent
silenced

Words too prosaic.
unless you whisper
"oh god."
or unless she screams it

But she wouldn't dare
shhhhh, you'll wake the children
shhhhh, you'll wake her soul
shhhhh you wake your own

But these fingers
though they struggle to type the right words
could move across lips and hearts
and the paper-thin skin of the wrist

With hot blue veins
throbbing in anticipation
of other things you
need or want

But they won't
desire is more, than some carnal thing
it is like a fire that ravages chaparral
driving the living things to refuge

And like whispering bells touched by smoke
the "fire followers"
erupting from the burnt blackness
little yellow blossoms of hope

As the conflagration sweeps
the mountains and valleys
the fingers trace her body
only in her dreams dancing in licks and lazy circles

Igniting fires
that germinate the seed of a woman hidden within
anointed by the smoke of destruction
and caressed by the flame to life again

She holds it all in
when she trembles
and galaxies on the other side of the universe
feel it too

But what she craves
is not just release but also restraint
arms wrapped around her to say
"you are finally safe"

A silly lock of hair
brushed gently back
from the forehead
as lips press again

Never satiated
if you really wanted to know
but was ever it enough
just to hold you?

Such is the way of sensory beings
building upon caress and embrace
heat and touch and taste
the feeling of safe and warm
ever sought and never found

And it all started with an errant thought
brought about by a stray wisp of hair
and a warm breeze
with the cool edge of a memory
or maybe a wish
or a dream

Kindness

The way you shuffled
the way you remembered me
when I wanted to forget
the way you washed your hair in the sink
the way you dressed for the Kingdom Hall

The way you dropped your head mid-conversation
to pray over every meal
awkward we'd sit mid-sentence
guilt resounding
because we did not pray like you

Sometimes you broke me
sometimes I hated your madness
it stung deeply in the recesses
of hidden truths

Like rulers across the feet
like chairs lodged under the doorknobs
like shoveling snow into heaps of anger and resentment
like mothers looking for love
and daughters too
I want to make you proud of me

Sometimes you were barreling into oblivion
and taking names along the way
but you were always harmless
innocent like a child
and I could see the bitterness
driving the madness
I knew the taste well

I always saw you
not with pity
but with familiarity
like a mirror

Then one day
you flew a thousand miles away
and my heart did break

Now I see
you flew away so you could live
and though I could hardly find the words
I cherished you
more mother to me than my own

You fed me
when you could hardly feed yourself
you provided the safety of shelter
and the warmth your sofa

You were grandmother to my boys
who always needed you more than you know
you loved them so well
you loved us so well
you did not fail us
and you did not leave us godless

I struggle to believe you are gone
I will forever feel the emptiness
of my mailbox as it never will hold again
re-purposed boxes
bearing rows of stamps
and a west-coast address

Full of pinecones and
old movies
bible tracts
and love

What Color are Your Eyes

What color are your eyes
what a silly question
what color is joy
what color is sorrow
there is a shade of green for each

And envy, and love and loneliness too
passion and sin and temptation
they beckon to you
-they want
and in truth there are too many colors in her eyes

Washed together
by too many years
her eyes the secret coordinates
to a universe
only she can navigate

The question is impossible to answer
for what color is Monday or Tuesday or Friday
what color is spring or autumn
what color is logic
or madness

What color is she
for that matter what color are you
you are one of her most sacred colors
you must know

After all, every ounce of her being is a verdant variant
if you pay attention to her eyes
you can discover the outline of her secrets
perhaps that is why she hides them from you

What color are your eyes
she laughs
they are all colors
and they are none

The River

I found peace
sitting by the river
tumbled stones
some sharp having only just
broken from yonder mountain
or smoothed by
the passage of time
etching away the scars
opposite, that of a woman
whose face has forgotten
what smooth feels like

The river always flows
like tears gathered up
and heaved down to the sea
all rivers lead there - eventually
and I found peace
sitting on a rock
surrounded by the wild

A dead fish
lodged upon the muddy bank
stared at me with one blank upturned eye

Did you just get old and die?
or perhaps some change by one degree
fragile thing that you are
I know who will rejoice in your carcass
this circle of life yields no empathy
and how foolish
we spend our days toiling for a deity
when the worms will feast in the end

Maybe the ghost that I am today
will meet the ghost I will be
over coffee
is it worth it?

The fat bellied worms cry, "yes!"

I'd rather sit and listen
to the song of the water
against the rocks that aren't me

I'd rather lean back and watch
birds make circles in the sky
wishing I could fly
wishing I could fly
wishing I could fly

The dead-eyed fish
could be my snack
or maybe
I'd just let it go

I found peace
sitting by the river
too chaotic and dirty and wild
too real
for the masses

They prefer the glow of their phones
to liquid gold flames of a sunset
reflecting upon cool water
or the opaque film-covered silver
of a dead fish-eye

Averting their gaze
they covet their things more
but I see and hear the whisper of the river
and no one will ever notice
until they find me
lodged upon the muddy bank
staring at you with one blank upturned eye

"What happened to her?" they ask
the worms smile

How a Soldier Hides

I imagine how a soldier hides
camouflage blending in with the jungle
or the desert or a concrete wall
I imagine but I cannot know
for I am not a soldier

I imagine his stealth
his restraint
box breathing
moving without sound

The man in his mirror
not so different
from the one you hunt
the one who hunts you

I imagine he is resolute
and when the deed is done
he slips away
proficient in arriving undetected
and leaving, the same

Situational awareness
trained to kill
although he never really wanted to kill
I imagine he wanted to love
but the war plan never allowed it

A lifetime will be spent
wondering why the algorithms and SOPs
never had provisions for brotherhood
or peace
or humanity
or trust
or forgiveness
not even a five-minute truce
for tea and civility

How does one win the heart
of such a hard thing?

But, I know
he is not so hard
he is soft and vulnerable
and aching for sweeter things
unspoken things
that modern warfare mocks

Of such customs and chivalry
lined upon fields of battle behind
the greatest guidon
with feathered plumes
and buttons of gleaming brass
against Prussian Blue
stoic faces and brave war cries
the opposite of stealth

They wore no camouflage
and their hearts
beat for passion
and for love
until they learned
they are more lethal
when they hide

Drowning

It takes a man an average of six minutes to drown
there's a scientific name for it
hypoxemia and irreversible cerebral anoxia
due to submersion in liquid

The act of drowning is reflexive
governed by the hindbrain
the primitive mind
that tells a man to run from a tiger
or wrestle a bear
fight or flight
kill or be killed

The body's instinctive response
to the act of drowning
is not conducive to survival
a man will do all the wrong things
which seems strange
a primordial biological rule
designed to kill a man
not save him
unless he can walk on water

Six minutes
give or take
awake
aware
frozen by fear
irrational
and dangerous

Assume the position
legs straight up and down
no supportive kick
arms out like an Oscar
only not gilded
head back in a silent cry to heaven
(no one hears you)

Fear
as lungs burn for air
does he pray?
pity, it's been a long time
but he remembers how
"our Father who art in heaven…"

He will die slow
like saying the rosary
as he struggles to live
reaching out for some unseen hand to rescue him
you can't really silence a silent scream
bubbles ascending
eyes supplicant in upward glassy stare
a fish swims by

He doesn't just slip away
he remains fully aware
'til he succumbs,
'til lungs fill with water
which is different from passing peacefully
now the real pain begins
the pain of dying

The fish swims closer
A curious sight
a boon for the fish
soon enough
but for a man
not so much
although some days
living feels awfully like drowning

Balloons

Sometimes a balloon is deflated
not because the air leaked out
of the openings into which it was filled
but because the body is full of holes
what then?

Bloodletting

Bloodletting
the humors flow
what is the life within?
without?
is it construct?
or black and white
calculated empirical coldness
void of emotion?

Red viscous clumps of blood cells
metallic iron rose upon alabaster skin
hungry for sun
the razor scores
the not so virgin, Virgin
too long untouched
to know warmth

Cold blade
and scarlet commingled
in warm water
held below soap bubbles
whose lies
pop, pop, pop
hiding toes, and rolls
and breasts with no more purpose

Succumbing to the
metaphor for the dead lump within
as it still drives the blood
through ventricle and atria
thunk thunk
thunk thunk
thunk thunk
dull and half dead
even before the cut

"Life" flows
dead eyes watch
as numb hand wipes the smear away
and covers the wound
with a generic beige bandage
nothing to see here

Spring has sprung
dead smiles among spent heads
of spring flowers
the perennial dead heads
dutifully pinched and tossed aside
as the pink water is circling down the drain

To Her Friend, The Poet

Perhaps you are drawn now to write about birds
I can't say I am not jealous
the raven at the door is terribly cliché
perhaps I wish you were standing still
in the crisp winter snow
gazing upon a different breast
watching her soar
because she desperately wants to

-fly

She'll return
quite dependably
to settle upon your branch
she's not a silly songbird
although she has a song to sing
but she doesn't feel seen
all the way up there

She is happenstance
borne of desire
yet only a little less invisible
than yesterday
selfish?
I presume
like trying to woo something
that doesn't want to be wooed

She's a caged crow
hanging from a hook on the wagon
of a traveling medicine man
he is trying to woo you too
with snake oil to sell
(when she's right she's right)
casual flip of the wrist

Oh but when she's wrong
she will never be allowed to forget it
fingers flapping in her face
storming with violence all around
pitchforks of resentment
nose to nose
for shame, for shame
she smells the hate on putrid breath

But the measured rhyme of the poet remains her calm
in case you didn't know why
she flies to you
-for you
in case you didn't know why
(she does)

She's no prop of Poe
just a boring old wounded migratory bird
plucking at refuse on the side of a road
you also happened to travel too

Not much, is she
unless you're looking
something
when you've nothing else
with which to compare

How do you even know to look?
how do you even see?
oh how Lucy laughs at me
but you, do write beautifully about birds
With speckled breasts

They seem to make you happy
they seem to calm your soul enough
to make marks on empty paper
and that is something special
after all

The Canvas

The canvas painted
is a fantasy
on the edge of a palette knife
caked with cheap acrylics
smeared with synthetic bristles
into the faux linen crosshatch
of bargain craft store pre-stretched "canvas"
the subject
driven by whatever mantra
the artist chanted into the water-speckled mirror
that morning

There's No Goddess of Hope

Eve was intuitive
aware and ashamed by her nakedness
she deceived herself
Cassandra she screams
at the stupid stars
and the stupid moon
as if they were once friends
they are deaf to her pleas
indifferent to her waning gibbous
she pretends they hear her
clinging to promises
never kept
a vapid fool
maybe this time it will be different?
and as for Artemis,
well, she will never learn
never listen to her inner self-whispering
trust no one and fade away to shadows
do not seek the hunter
or you will surely suffer
at the end of his shaft
after all there is no goddess of hope

Hiraeth

I was struck by this word today
while preening through a crossword
that was too advanced, I know
optimistically embarked upon all the same

Hiraeth, a Welsh word
you'll find neither Roget or Webster claims
a spiritual longing for a home
that never was

Or mayhap yet to come
I don't know
it fits well into my storylines
like familiar whispers in my dreams

Hiraeth catches the eye
blows through my hair like
the breeze
and flows in with my breath

Some humble thing
like a fancy
giving large for small reasons
yet longing for more

A certain type of screw
for a certain type of turning
knowing what tool you need
but also knowing the tool does not exist

Perhaps Hiraeth is the invention
the inspiration
that drives a dreamer (or the screw)
to some unknown destination

Perhaps Hiraeth is why
I sit on bridges
and watch the currents flow
hoping I won't jump
this time

Leaving ancestors further removed
from kith, from kin
if even only through a middling exhale
of haunted remembrance

Hiraeth is perhaps how I know
the intimacy of the reflection of a tree
undulating across the shallows of my river
how the light plays in the dark bends
of the flow of my soul

O'er a lifetime I've stood guardian
o'er what never belonged to me
not my home
not my heart
perhaps Hiraeth just- is
the universe forbidden

Casting my own shadow
divining the autumn leaves
as they float along eddy and swirl
like whimsy to a faraway sea

Something calls
the melody sounds like trust
wrapped in a minor chord of melancholy
eyes closed too tight
as she whispers
I cannot bleed for thee

Hiraeth
perhaps my own shortcomings
playing against conscience

For I have always been homeless
in the most rhetorical sense
having never belonged to a home
or a home having never belonged to me

Keening agony
to not know my ancestors
or my story
to be rootless
to be motherless

The cover by which my book is judged
is spittle dubbed "whiteness"
devoid of culture
the wrong sort of suffering

No pedigree
no father's father's name
great mother's silent claim
I am as nothing as nothing can be

Perhaps Hiraeth is
the void between the physical
and the constructs of the mind
not a tangible tactile refuge
or the promise of respite

A safe haven
sounds real nice
wanted and warm
intimately welcomed

Ancestors to be loved and
cherished and remembered
yarns spun into fine silk tapestries
for swaddling babes warmed by the fire
around which our stories are told

Perhaps Hiraeth is neither ruled
by carnal pleasures
nor abandoned by them
wanting to be touched
such rightness
and a sigh of contentment

Hiraeth
a longing for a home
that may not be

yet

Or a home we know we've already lost
watching it slip through our fingers
into dumpsters on the curb
and still, we can't see that one damn good thing
before us
for the taking

Hiraeth
a longing
I guess I'm glad to have stumbled upon
but maybe in truth
I've always known
I belong anywhere but here

Tick Tock

Sometimes the ticking of the clock
taunts me
as I cling desperately
to each hour
as it bleeds into another day
each breath more meddling
as if I had the right
screams silenced and swallowed
by the tick, tick, tick

This is what empty feels like
or humility?
no –
humiliation

Impasto

Impasto: from the Italian word *impastare*
(be sure to roll the "r")
which means to knead
as in dough
which is not the same as to need

Impasto is painting with thick paint
on boar's bristle
or painting with a palate knife
of cold stainless steel

By definition
undefined

Bold color builds unblended
the eye discerns the intended form
as light plays in dips and valleys
bathed in the glossy sheen of sweet linseed
the medium becomes sculpture
and dimension

Imagine touching
the texture and groove
left by the bristles of van Gogh
imagine touching
his very soul

For centuries the masters pondered
the physics of painting
the geometry of art
on two dimensional planes
chiaroscuro
sfumato
l'ultima cena.

When realism gave way to emotion
they abandoned the lines
and the cherubic babes
the naked breasts of the Virgins
surrendered to a different kind of
passion

Color and whimsy
darkness and pain
debauchery
lust
pressed into linen, stretched tight
to the edge of madness
pressed by the knife
by Intelligent Design

For impasto
requires faith
you will see
the sorrow and secret
in the eye
the untamed mountain
in the distance
the petulant petal
of the wildflower
the delicate curve of her breast
beating for you

Impasto by definition
is substance
not flat
rather, elevated

Pinks in a blue sky
that caress the cypress trees
strokes so dense
they might still be uncured

And so the humble girl
who wandered a museum
in the shadow of the masters
will paint too
pressing her oils into canvas
and calling it art

Maybe someday
a random soul
may want to reach out
to touch her
impasto

Anatomy of the Heart

The heart
a unique bundle of specialized cardiac muscles
bound by the rib cage like an incarcerated thing
for the most part, independent of the brain

Ruled over by a cult of mysticism
a conspiracy of feelings
a cabal of moral indignation
a doctrine of navigation
follow your heart, they say

If one must navigate the wrinkled map of my heart
in order to find my treasure
they might find the parchment
stinks of wasted time
opportunity and abuse

My heart has none of the charm
of Hereford's map
although I too have dangerous places
on my fringes

My heart has none of the charm
of Mercator's map
I fear no explorer will ever
navigate me

But still I wonder
is there treasure?

The anatomical drawing of the heart
more closely resembles
the sterility of a flowchart
than two whimsical mucronate bumps

A complex twining of ventricles and atria
valves and chambers
that ache when they remember
the sound of your voice

Simple
mechanical
scientific

The bottom of my heart
resembles a sharp terminal point
like the tip of a knife
like the spine of a porcupine

Like thorns on a blackberry bramble
that tear at the flesh of your arms and legs
when all you want is the burst of something warm and sweet
to take away the bitter salt of the tears

You can't embrace
caress or snuggle
such a hostile thing
and you can't reach the ripest fruit

The heart is a simple pump
with unidirectional flow
arrows and lines labeled
with meticulous manuscript
in da Vinci's anatomy book

Recirculation
never ceasing
every day, every hour, every second
rate and rhythm and pressure
osmosis,
homeostasis
repeat

The heart is ruled by magnetism
nodes with Latin names like sinus, atrial, ventricular
the heart controls itself independent of the brain
and the brain - it does meddle

The nodes never stop
pumping out positive ions
until they do
every day, every hour, every second
until flat line
and then the worms rejoice

Push and push and push
a peculiar property of positive little polar soldiers
pushing each other around
their little polar world

Closed circuit like the battery in your smart phone
obedient like blinking cursors
which stinks of conformity
and whatever else society feeds you

The heart triggers
thousands of chemical explosions each day
80-120 microscopic transactions per minute
if you're not too fat
too old
too everything

Easy to manipulate with
coke
smoke
platitudes

All of my positives line up
looking for negative counterparts
like a puzzle seeks a receiving piece
casting their positive charges across
a dead lump of tough flesh
too fibrous to make a good cut of meat

Did you ever notice how
an army of positive ions
can resemble the crucifix

God is good?

Or maybe
floating about
tilted on their sides
they resemble an x

Does x mark the spot?

Or maybe they are just saying
please stop
you're not welcome here
you positive bitch

Niosh F2000-13

I know how you died on Valentine's Day
shit hit the fan
and fast
you knew all along
that you never had control
you exchanged your life
for a fast food joint
no lives to save but your own
poor wager
a life for a greasy terracotta floor
that smells of quarter-pounders

You only wanted to breathe
and you fought like hell
and you knew- as we all do
no cavalry was coming
you laughed that laugh
we all laugh
when hope is lost
and dark humor is all you have
you laughed as you succumbed
after all, you were the fucking cavalry

There is no one to rescue the rescuer
and not everybody goes home
after the embers cooled
they sifted through
and found your charred remains
better late than never
I guess

Now a report bears your name

Firefighter #2

(Kimberly)
your story is told in data and metrics
while your brothers sleep
with expanding guts and bushy mustaches
grasping tightly to their bourbon bottles
praying the back and knees and mind
make it to 55 before the cancer gets them

```
"She was found entangled in wires and a
pair of wire cutters (believed to be hers)
were found nearby."
```

You should have never been there
the tribe still resents your lady parts
but you showed them
that we all die the same
a few feet from your captain
wire cutters in hand
to free yourself from the entrapment
inches from the door
no radio for the mayday (budget cuts)
in the back kitchen
of the Mac fucking Donald's

Arson?
murder?
for what?

```
"Cause of death for both victims was
asphyxia due to smoke inhalation"
```

I know how you died
I feel the anxiety of it every time I bottle up
I want to whisper to you

It's alright, the captain pulled his regulator off too

Your fate was never a weakness of your double x
it is a weakness of human instinct
I hope the chicken nuggets were saved along with the egos

```
"Ladder 68 found the victim, who was
identified as victim #1 (Lewis), with his
SCBA face piece donned, but his regulator
not connected. His SCBA air cylinder
harness was partially removed and entangled
in wires."
```

You knew it would kill you quicker is all
did you know the door was close enough
to be cold metal on your gloved fingertips?
(assuming you'd kept your gloves on)

Victims #1 and #2
you have no tribe
no holiday
the free cups of coffee stopped
not long after 9/11
you have the bell strike of 5-5-5
returning to quarters
and your memory fades as fast as the last reverberation
of the last strike of the case brass
end of shift

We will salute you as you pass beneath bridge
we will remember you at Emmitsburg
then enshrine you forever
in a NIOSH report a lesson of what not to do
while the next generation of the ovarian handicapped
will learn the hard way to do it faster, longer, harder
and never know your name

But we are all you
training to rescue ourselves
fighting the urge to rip off the mask
whether a pistol in the mouth (Kenny)
a rope around the neck (Brianna)

a needle in the arm (Mick)
covid (Dickie)
or some prick with a Molotov cocktail (Kimberly and Lewis)
and the list goes on
because we all die the same in the end

Senior Living Shades of Green

I am sorry I forgot your name
even though I wrote it down on the form
and I typed it into the database
for the bean counters
your death quantified
to calculate how many 4x4 bandages
I didn't use
or the contrived cost
of carrying the jump bag
to the first floor
third door on the right

I remember this because
the smell was evident
as we crossed through the lobby
appointed with vinyl armchairs
and fake flowers
and some perversion of Bach lullabies
for the other end of life

Two weeks
dead in your bed
covers pulled up under your chin
so peacefully sleeping

Your dog lost
sole companion in this world
as you grew old and obsolete
the poster on the counter
pleads for his return

How does one lose a dog
in a senior living apartment complex?
how does on lay dead in their bed for two weeks
with no one wondering where you are
if you're ok?
what that smell is?

Don't touch a thing
a grandmother's living room
now a crime scene
I hadn't even seen you yet
in the back room
but I knew what I would find there

And there you were
a shade of green I did not anticipate
two weeks dead
the maggots already matured
spiders spinning webs in the sink
to catch the flies
that were born in your gut and flesh
they always find a way in

Empty dog dish on the floor
empty medicine bottles on the counter
all of the labels too new

Two weeks dead in your bed
you thought you were alone
but I know you, I am you
I am sorry I forgot your name

Reverberation

Reverberation:
the prolongation of a sound
like your laughter the last time I ever saw you
sitting on my couch
a surprise visit
and you with all of your infinite knowledge
a damn titan
told me you were done
your body was done
you said you were scared

How can you
a leathery, hardened smoke eater
a fucking legend among all firemen
even know fear?

Thumbs up, one eye closed
"big fire, big water, small fire, small water
don't over think it"
you taught me well
(god, I'm fucked)
you laughed it off
in that signature country boy giggle
that made you seem simple

And you were
dump truck to the quarry
fire truck to the fire
dogs to the creek
repeat for 40 years

I still hear you laughing on my sofa
I miss you.
you were better than me

Reverberation:
a continuing effect
a repercussion
that ache in my chest
that started with a simple social media post

"fuck"

Not too much digging and I found the source
You
ICU
ventilator

fuck

Three days later
gone
goddamn this virus
didn't it know you're a fucking titan?
a legend
my hero
my friend
(and I liked you…)

Reverberation:
calculated by some measure of time
and decay relative to the speed of sound
the size of the room and absorption

But your laughter in my head
and the pain of your loss
defies the laws of physics
my heart and head
hold the memory as it ricochets
to infinity

I find myself walking
along the boardwalk tonight
with a cool breezes
full of ghosts

But mostly you
a path we once walked together
my first time
30 years ago
and did we did laugh

I was wide-eyed and new
and you were a leathery
hardened smoke eater
a fucking legend among all firemen
and we were invincible

but now you are gone

fuck

Flowers

What do you think
goes through the mind of a flower
that blooms for only one day
as she stretches out her petals

Aandblom with a bright heart of gold
humble among dry prairie grasses
purest white with blush of pink violet

Like Lucy
half hidden with a smile
most will never see
she dances gently in the breeze
all of the bees come to visit her
and buzz sweetly in her ear

They tell her she is beautiful
and she stretches further
is there more?

Her roots delve deeper
and there they do not find more
the earth is too dry
compacted like arid concrete
parched like the skin of an old woman
a lattice of jagged cracked bricks of clay
eager for a drink of water

Finding no quench for her thirst
she shrinks back
embarrassed for the act
of wanting to be more

Her pinks begin to fade
and the grains of her soul
fall in yellow dust
like desiccated tears
sprinkled upon the soil below

A lost generation
the broken limb of the family tree
Enola
Bella
name unknown

Maybe someday
another flower will grow
from her tears
but for her
the bees no longer come
the sun no longer shines
and in the dark
she blooms her brightest
and how she does shine
this one last time
'til she fades for eternity

Should she smile at the memory
of the warm glow of the sun on her petals
or is her story a tale of woe
every day ending in a broken faded smile,
every moment unquenched regret
as she turns gray
like dried prairie grass
as each evening
she dies anew

Succumbed, she lays flat
another layer
of hard packed clay
waiting to crack in the glare of high noon

I guess it's perspective
she should be happy
for her twelve hours of glory
any good flower would be
Lucy would agree

Gardenias

My scent is that of gardenias
a not so humble evergreen
and related to coffee
rubiaceous
and so very sweet
a thing I longed to be
with beautiful blooms
reminiscent of jasmine
but not so dignified
intoxicating
like vanilla
and the smell of green
if green had smell
which is not to say
I am intoxicating
but merely that my scent
is that of gardenias

My mother is fragrance
free and clear
not even the color of Gray
whereas I was always too multi-dimensional for her
if I did not have her nose
I'd wonder how I could even be
her daughter
alas, with her nose
I worship scents
not sense
how she resented that

My father appreciated beautiful things
he always smelled of coffee
he knew I cherished the gardenias
and by happenstance
there came to be one humble bush
in his backyard
it came with the house
among the azaleas

and rhododendron
his refuge, solace among the berms
his favorites

I never lived there
this was never my home
they never even noticed it was there
until I noticed
humble and in the shade
of the proper southern porch
with coved ceiling
and lazy fans
that stir mosquitos, gnats and guilt
around in the soup
of high Georgia summer

I caught their familiar scent first
c'est déjà fait
I followed it
to the corner
of the garden
humble bush, with white blooms

My mother
on the other hand
was glad I'd found the source
of the foul stench
and she ordered it removed
I begged him not to
and maybe he knew
his mother loved them too

My grandmother
was named after a humble shrub
a soft forest carpet
-Ferne
deeply misunderstood
far too principled
and set in her ways

With a sharp tongue and keen eye
for weakness from across the dinner table
a pioneer in a man's world
like me
her legacy within me
she had a love of old things
and names
like a child named Enola
that never was

Gardenias come in varieties
white waxy blooms that
symbolize purity
sweet buttery yellows
for sweet memories and dreams
red is rare
secret love or joy
which seems contrary to me
I don't even believe in love

My father's gardenia was white
and he was pure
I am not

And you?
What is your scent?
I imagine it is man and sweat
and hard work
that sometimes masks tears

Or musk of the forest
gunpowder and knife oil
starched uniforms
the smell of government green
coffee and juniper soap

Or the longing for hardwood smoke
from an old stone hearth
settled upon a tribal rug
sipping tea from a chipped cup

Pipe tobacco and ink
on fresh crisp unmarked paper
and whatever else you fancy

But you don't fancy gardenias
and you don't fancy me
after all
you said it is never a good idea
to wear florals
in the heat of summer

Morning Glories

One morning so very long ago
a little girl plucked a morning glory from a vine
clinging to the weathered planks
of the privacy fence that enclosed a small backyard
in the suburbs, somewhere

Morning glories are complex
people either love them or hate them
they are invasive
practically a weed
like poison ivy without the itch

Their progeny blow in on the breeze
and they populate uninvited
to choke the hibiscus and the rose
and the prized blue hydrangeas

Neither majestic
like the haughty rhododendron
nor painted in bucolic scenes
save lesser studies by Delacroix or O'Keefe

Frida knew
They bloomed at dawn from her breast
to fall off of the life-giving vine
to wither and die by nightfall
the truncated life of a tortured bloom

A life too short
yet the wild and twisted trunk
from which it sprung lives on
it doesn't seem fair

Father loved azaleas anyhow
azaleas prefer the shade
while a morning glory
craves the light

Morning glories
captivated the little girl's innocent eyes
still wide open to the possibility
and the purity of purple

She believed
in the promise of morning
and that flowers should be picked
not knowing that doing so was to watch it fade

Cut off from its root
deprived of nutrients
no longer supported by the bond with the vine
plucked off it was meant to die

slow
sad
and alone

The girl didn't place it in a glass
to pretend it still lived
instead she wrapped it a soft napkin
the kind folded over into four thin squares
and stamped with fruit or words like
laugh
love
family

A pulp based outtake
of what happiness is supposed to be
more like rote compost-able lies
you tell yourself each day

She carefully wrapped her bloom
as she waited for the bus
a yellow and black institutional yawn

She settled upon
the sticky dark green pleather
she cradled her fragile prize
against the abrupt jerks
and lurches
and jerks and jeers

Her idea was not to keep
such a prize for herself
rather it was a gift
to her teacher
a tribute

Maybe then she'd like her
maybe then she'd see her
even as a child she knew
kindness and friendship
must be leveraged
must be bought

But the morning glory has secrets
they make you see things that never were
make it safe to dream
and they only bloom for the sun.

When the girl presented her "gift"
the teacher found a closed off
sad dead thing
wilted against pale tissue

The girl quickly hid her shame
hoping no one noticed her smile
had faded
like her bloom

Her eyes welled up
with barely restrained tears
and she ran for solitude of
a bathroom stall

She learned she cannot trust
a beautiful thing
for they always wither
and die

Some sooner than others
some before the first coffee cools in the cup
for the bloom was always
only an illusion,

She'd absorbed the toxin
of an untouchable weed
that never existed for her
in the first place

The Mountain

Far away
rising from the lazy azure
tumbled stony shore
reach'd out like arms
to Ionian and Aegean
brothers and foes
steppingstones of the gods?
or merely haunting cuneate shadows
iconic purple haze
when gazed upon from
ancient Khios

Dreams from afar
aloft sweet sea-salty spray
the smell of turquoise and glassy greens
amid juniper and oleander
myrtle and pine
cyprus scrubbed low by crystalline breeze
scorched by the summer sun
like his heart, scorched by a woman
brush strokes of hostile ochre and sienna clay
unwilling to yield to root or seed
without coaxing

And nestled in the crook of the steep rise
he stands before his mountain
feet warmed on the sunbaked shore
whilst blue tourmaline shimmers
awash'd in celestial rhythm
between ancient grains of sand
and murmur'd thrum and sigh
to each rolling surge and seaward flow
smooth steps lead to limestone and loulaki
as the thatch coved veranda casts shadows
over damp footprints absorbed by terracotta clay

There she finds him
sweet with ocean and salt
sun soaked into his skin
that chased away
purple sunken shallow eyes
that had never known peace
chained by the sins of his fathers
and his own.
now cloaked in pale spun linen
worries evaporating
like footprints seeping into his birthright
the man who was
becomes the man who is free
but alone

Peppered with ancient history
the waves lap gently onto gravelly shore
knowing what blood and violence tasted like
pebbles rich with golden-hued memories
of quartz and moss-colored feldspar
black volcanic glass
challenging phalo blues
for the definition of somber
remembrance of the violence of fiery rendering
shimmering in contrast to the indifferent cerulean sky
uncommitted save for a wandering cloud

I imagine him standing upon the shore
wind in his hair
crisp shirt fluttering against bronze jaw
that long ago abandoned the soldier's blade
he waited for his friend
and she did arrive
as if she stepped off a breeze
or a dream
and she slip'd her cool hand into his
pulling him into embrace
and she sighed

Tide at their feet
she rests beside him
demanding nothing
tracing the lines of his face
as if she could unlock the ancient uncial
script of his life
as if she could unlock the codex of his heart
and he turned his eyes against her again
her gentle siege repelled
as a single tear dried on the lashes
before it even hit her cheek

Regret or resolve
he trusts she will hold him again
her eyes close and she pulls away
like a sea-bound flow that vows to return
and he too fades
into the cuneate shadows
of iconic purple haze
lost in dreams of blue upon pebbles
and ever in the shadow of his mountain

Erica Elizabeth Gray is a special education teacher and a thirty-year veteran Firefighter from Montgomery County, Maryland. In 2015, Erica earned a Bachelor of Science in Elementary Special Education from Mount Saint Mary's University and recently completed a Master of Science in Applied Behavior Analysis. She plans to embark on her next adventure in research and outreach to bring attention to and reduce line-of-duty deaths and suicide in first responders. When she is not teaching, she can be found staffing the engine, rescue squad or ambulance at her local volunteer fire department or playing tenor saxophone in her local community college jazz ensemble. She currently resides in Shepherdstown, West Virginia with her husband, raising two teenage sons and working on her next books.

www.ingramcontent.com/pod-product-compliance
Lightning Source LLC
Chambersburg PA
CBHW071730090426
42738CB00011B/2446